The Girls' Book of Spells

Rachel Elliot

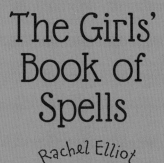

ARCTURUS

SAFETY FIRST!

★ Always place candles on a flameproof dish or in a candle holder.
★ Ask an adult to help you light candles or incense.
★ Only use matches if you have the permission of an adult.
★ Never leave candles unattended or fall asleep while one is alight.
★ Always ask an adult to help you if you feel unsure about a spell.
★ While you are casting spells, make sure that you are somewhere safe and that an adult is nearby who knows where you are.
★ Be careful in handling all your spell supplies and tools.
★ Never put yourself in danger or do a spell too quickly.

ARCTURUS

This edition published in 2023 by Arcturus Publishing Limited
26/27 Bickels Yard, 151–153 Bermondsey Street,
London SE1 3HA

ISBN: 978-1-83940-423-8
CH000571US
Supplier 29, Date 0623, PI 00004219

Author: Rachel Elliot
Cover illustrator: Luna Valentine
Illustrator: Robyn Neild
Editor: Kate Overy

Printed in China

Contents

Introduction

Since time began, certain special girls across the globe have dreamed of altering and improving the world around them. You are one of those magical girls, and that is why you have picked up this book.

What this book can do for you

To draw on the unseen forces of the universe, you must be grounded. This means staying down to earth and clear-sighted, and never losing touch with reality. It also means that you need a basic knowledge of what magic is (and what it is not).

This book will guide your first steps along the path, giving you the basic information you need and a few simple spells to get you started.

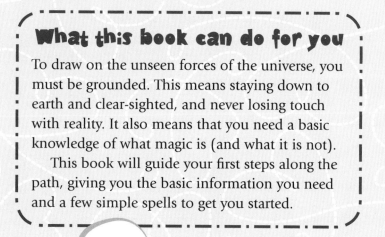

How to use this book

Read carefully through the first pages. You will learn what spells are, how to prepare for spellcasting, and most importantly, the rules of sorcery. Good luck and happy spellcasting!

What are spells?

Spells are a way of drawing on the strength of the unseen forces that exist within the universe, using a combination of words and actions, as well as the power of your own mind.

It is very difficult to define magic, because there has never been a definition that everyone would agree with, but one thing is certain—there is magic inside everyone just waiting to be unleashed!

Magical you

It is incredibly important to know yourself before you begin spellcasting. What kind of person are you? What are your strengths and weaknesses? What is your place in the world around you? When you know and understand yourself, the power of your own mind and personality will help you to create positive, strong spells. This is because the strongest magic comes from inside you. Spells are the creations of your inner character and most heartfelt wishes.

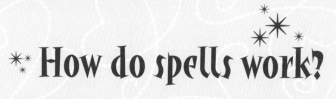

How do spells work?

Human beings have great powers, but we have forgotten how to use them. By focusing our minds through the use of spells, we can tap into the unseen power of the universe and ask it to help us achieve our goals.

However, just as we have the power to do good, we also have the power to do harm. In harming others, we harm ourselves and warp our own nature. It is supremely important that you should never cast a spell, no matter how good it is, for or on another person—unless they have asked you to do it for them or have given you their permission.

What goes around comes around

Any negative spell you cast can come back on you with triple the power. So it's quite simple—if you cast a harmful spell, you will only end up harming yourself.

Several things have to come together to make a spell work properly:

1 The correct materials and supplies

Just as when you are making a cake, you need to use the right ingredients to get the result you want from your spell. The better the quality of your materials, the better the quality of your spell.

2 The time of the spell

Some spells should be cast at a particular time of day. Some need the mystical power of the moon; others require the refreshing energies of dawn.

3 The state of mind of the spellcaster

Your mood will have an effect on the spell you are casting. It could change the intention of the spell or stop it from working at all. You should be calm and grounded when you are spellcasting.

4 The will of the unseen powers of the universe

By casting a spell, you are asking for the unseen powers of the universe to help you achieve your aim. In order for your spell to work, those energies must be willing to assist you.

5 The correct spell

If, for example, you want to protect an object, it's essential to use a spell for protection rather than casting a spell for luck. Make sure that you have picked the best spell to achieve your aims.

There is a code of behavior that a sorceress should hold at the core of every spell she casts. This guidance is very important, because it will help you to learn how to cast a spell safely, wisely, and well.

A relaxing meditation will put you in a good frame of mind in which to cast a spell. It will also help you with challenges you might be facing in life.

Preparing for the art of spellcasting

Below is a simple meditation. If you have never meditated before, this is a good basic meditation to start with.

1 Go outside and find a quiet, safe place where you can sit down.

2 Close your eyes, and think about your sense of touch. How does the breeze feel on your face? Is your skin being warmed by the sun or made wet from the rain?

3 Now listen to the sounds around you. Focus on one at a time, concentrating on natural sounds such as birdsong, rather than cars or sirens.

4 Next, use your sense of smell. Again, try to focus on natural smells, such as flowers and earth.

5 Finally, be aware of all three senses at once. Put your senses at the center of your mind, and let everything else flow away.

Grounding yourself

It can be dangerous to perform a spell without first having grounded yourself. Grounding yourself keeps you in your reality and protects you from dangerous energies. You must focus on the world around you and acknowledge your place within it.

Steps to stay grounded

There are many ways to ground yourself, and as you learn more about spellcasting, you will discover more of them. But to get you started, here is a simple grounding routine.

1 Sit still with both feet on the floor, parallel and about 20 centimeters/8 inches apart.

2 Imagine that there are roots coming out of your feet and growing downward, deep into the earth like tree roots.

3 Visualize yourself connecting with the earth.

4 Speak the words on the next page.

★

I value and respect the unseen powers of the universe.
Each day I try to understand them more clearly.
I ask for strength and support.
I ask for the wisdom to understand
and the strength to forgive.

★

I will only ask the energies of the universe to work for good.
I do not wish to harm any living thing.

★

Those powers belong to the universe,
and I am part of the universe.
I am part of the strength and the power,
but the strength and the power do not belong to me.
I belong to the universe.
I am part of the universe.

★

Learning to focus

Everyone has trouble paying attention sometimes. We switch off. We only listen to half the words. We skip the boring parts! But when you're calling upon unseen energies, without focus, your spells can go wrong.

Focus on yourself

★ To know your true self, including your strengths and weaknesses, you have to be honest with yourself.

★ Every single person in the world makes mistakes or thinks unkind thoughts sometimes.

★ No one else knows what you are thinking—they only know what you say and what you do. So be truthful with yourself, and face your weaknesses as well as valuing your strengths.

★ Don't forget—sometimes a strength can be a weakness, and a weakness can be a strength.

Focus on those around you

★ Listen to what people say and what they don't say. Practice paying attention to their hopes, wishes, fears, and loves.

★ Look them in the eyes when they are speaking to you. Are their eyes happy or sad? Honest or untruthful? Kind or hurtful? Peaceful or in pain?

★ The more you try to understand other people's feelings, the more effective your spells will be.

★ Put your trust and faith in others. Often, if you expect someone to be kind, they will be.

Focus on the moment

★ Do not think about what happened yesterday or what will happen tomorrow.

★ Remember your meditation technique? To focus on the moment, concentrate on everything you know about this particular moment in time.

Where are you?

What is the weather like?

Are you warm or cool?

What sounds can you hear?

What colors and shapes can you see?

What can you smell?

Improving your ability to focus will help you to:

★ Identify the right spell for any situation.

★ Understand how to help the people around you.

★ Recognize truth, strength, and wisdom.

Physical and spiritual harmony

Your physical self and your spiritual self change and develop. As you grow, your physical self gets taller, your feet get bigger, your hair gets longer, and your body gets stronger. Your spiritual self grows, too, but it's up to you how much it grows.

★ You can touch your hands and your face, your legs and your hair. This is your physical self.
★ You can't touch your ideas and your opinions, your loves and your hopes. This is your spiritual self.
★ Both are you, but other people can only see the physical you. They can't see the spiritual you.

Your body stops growing when you reach a certain age, but your spiritual self keeps growing until you choose to stop. It is always ready to learn more and develop further. The more your spiritual self learns, the kinder and wiser it will become, and the better and stronger your spells will be.

Making spells happen

By now, you know that to make spells happen, you need some materials, the right words, and you need the correct place and time. All these things are the job of your physical self. But the most important part of making spells happen takes place inside you—and this is the job of your spiritual self.

Both your physical and spiritual selves deserve attention and care. Your physical self needs food, water, warmth, shelter, exercise, and play. Your spiritual self needs guidance, love, support, kindness, forgiveness, and trust.

If your physical and spiritual selves are in harmony, you will feel happy, confident, and relaxed. There may be days where you feel sad or worried that your mind is not "whole." Spells can help you with this, but the first stage is to be in balance. Without that, you won't be able to make successful spells happen.

The rules of enchantment

There are rules by which you must abide if you want to become a good sorceress. Read through the words of the rules of enchantment opposite. This is the promise that you must make, and you must be sure that you understand and mean every word before you make the promise. Remember that any negative spell you cast can come back on you threefold, so your spellcasting should only be used for good.

The promise

When you are ready, prepare to make the promise. You should shower or take a bath, and let your hair dry naturally. Dress yourself in your spellcasting clothes (see page 33). Then find a quiet, safe place (like your bedroom) where you will not be interrupted.

Look into a mirror and into your own eyes. Focus on all you know about your physical self. Think about the color of your hair, eyes, and skin. Meditate on the shape of your fingers, your height, and your shape.

Keep looking deep into your eyes, and think about your spiritual self. Focus on your strengths and weaknesses, your hopes and plans. Then speak the words of the promise (opposite).

The sorceress promise

I ask my physical self and my spiritual self to exist in harmony.
I ask for the strength and wisdom to keep them balanced.
I will not neglect the needs of my body for the sake of my spirit.
I will not neglect the needs of my spirit for the sake of my body.
I will work hard to help my spiritual self grow.

★

I ask for the wisdom to listen to the needs of others.
I ask that my understanding will grow and widen all my life.

★

I will not cast a spell to harm another.
I will not cast a spell to make another behave,
feel, or think in any way against their will.
I will not cast a spell for or on anyone else unless
they know about it and have asked for or allowed it.
I will never cast a spell when I am angry or unforgiving.

★

I will develop a calm state of mind in which to cast spells.
I will train my mind to think of all people in the light of love
and forgiveness.

★

This is my promise.

Spell Supplies

There are many different oils, candles, and stones that can be used in spellcasting, and it takes time to build up your collection. Don't expect to be able to get everything all at once—most sorceresses need years to develop a really broad collection. Try saving a little pocket money each month toward your spell supplies.

Top Tip:
Look in alternative remedy stores, crystal sellers, and gift shops for supplies, or check online retailers for a wider choice.

Types of magic

There are several types of magic, and you will prefer some to others. Different types of magic work best for different types of spells.

Here are some of the basic types you will learn to use in this book.

Elemental

The four elements of air, earth, fire, and water can give extra energy to your spells, because each has its own focus and force.

Color

Color can deeply affect moods and emotions. Schools are often painted bright colors, and few people paint the walls in their homes a dark color, because they find it depressing. Use color in your spells to complement your goal.

Herbal

Herbs are often used in pouches or bags to make talismans (see below). There are many different herbs available for different purposes.

Candle

Candles can be used in magic to symbolize yourself and your intentions. Burn one while you are meditating to strengthen the success of your spell.

Crystal

Every precious stone has its own power and characteristic. Crystals store energy and have their own vibrations. For these reasons, they are often used in healing spells.

Binding

A rope, string, or ribbon can represent the intention of your spell. Tying knots in it helps to declare your goal, bind your spell, and keep it working.

Talismans

These are charms or amulets that are given power through the casting of a spell, and they are usually made to bring good luck or protection.

Candles

The type and color of candle you need depends of the purpose of your spell. Candles should be unused and "charged" at the start of a spell, then used safely.

Candle types

Table candles are the most basic type and should stand in candlesticks.

Taper candles are tall, thin, and fragile. Use them when casting a spell that requires a fast outcome.

Tea light candles are tiny and ideal for spells that need a candle to burn out.

Pillar candles are thick and do not need a candlestick, but you should always place them on a flat candleholder.

Candle colors

Different colors have different meanings. Choose your candle color carefully, since it can affect your spell.

✳ White—purity, truth seeking, and peace ✳ Purple—hidden truths and psychic powers ✳ Blue—wisdom and protection ✳ Brown—friendship and support ✳ Orange—fairness and justice ✳ Pink—romance and caring ✳ Green—healing and growth ✳ Red—passion and strength ✳ Gold—success and happiness ✳ Yellow—imagination and intelligence ✳ Silver—dreams and intuition

How to charge a candle

1 Charge candles before each spell. First, sit in a quiet, safe place, and hold the candle with both hands.

2 Take deep breaths, and focus on your goal.

3 Think about the energy of the universe. Imagine it flowing into your body and mixing with your own personal energy.

4 Allow the mixed energy to flow through your hands and into the candle.

5 Say the following words:

I charge this candle with energy and power.

May it burn with a strong flame and work for good.

6 Strike a match above the candle, and light the wick.

7 Allow the candle to burn as you cast your spell.

Candle signs

✳ The flame burns evenly—the spell will succeed.

✳ The flame is weak—someone is trying to block your spell.

✳ The flame burns well and then gives off some smoke—the spell will work well at first, but other problems might arise.

✳ The flame gives off smoke at first but then burns well—things will seem difficult at first, but they will improve.

✳ The flame goes out before the spell is complete—you are not using an appropriate spell.

The natural world

Spellcasting works best when natural ingredients are used. This is because these ingredients are part of the world in the same way that we are, and so our energies are more closely in tune.

Herbs and flowers

Many spells use herbs; each one has its own unique qualities and powers. It would take a whole book to list them all, but here are some plants that can be useful for each of the categories in this book.

✳ **Home:** camomile, lavender, aloe, gardenia, black pepper, nettle ✳ **School:** rosemary, lily of the valley, vanilla, walnut ✳ **Friends:** lemon, rose, passionflower ✳ **Luck:** apple, hazel, holly, ivy, mint, rowan ✳ **Love:** basil, ginger, honeysuckle, jasmine, mistletoe

Oils

Oils are used not only in spells but also in bathing. Here are some basic essential oils and their qualities.

✳ **Oils for energy:** lemon, basil, peppermint
✳ **Oils for harmony:** myrrh, neroli, sandalwood
✳ **Oils for love:** cinnamon, ylang-ylang, clary sage
✳ **Oils for wisdom:** frankincense, nutmeg, rosemary

Trees

Natural objects such as trees are a vital part of magic, so it is important that you should understand their meanings and powers.

Go for a walk around your home, and look at the trees and plants that grow nearby. To be a true sorceress, you will need a good understanding of the powers and qualities of trees. Here are some of the most familiar.

The magic of trees

Apple—love and healing
Birch—caring and nurturing
Blackthorn—wisdom and protection
Cedar—life
Elder—protection
Elm—love
Fir—birth
Hawthorn—protection and marriage
Hazel—wisdom and communication
Holly—sleep and luck
Ivy—mystery and marriage
Oak—strength and courage
Willow—imagination
Yew—protection and renewal

 Crystals

You will feel more of a natural connection to certain crystals, and you should make a talisman bag to hold those that are most special. Let your instinct draw you to the crystals that are meant for you.

There is a great deal to learn about the power of crystals, so understanding their strengths and meanings is a good place to start.

How crystals can help your spells

Choose stones that represent the four natural elements:

Clear or yellowish stones for air
Red, orange, or black for fire
White, blue, or turquoise for water
Green or brown for earth

Crystals and their powers

Agate: grounding, success, and good fortune

Aventurine: creativity, health, and good luck

Carnelian: peace, bravery, and safety for travelers

Citrine: spiritual wisdom, courage, and self-confidence

Clear quartz: spirituality, love, and healing

Hematite: grounding, spiritual development, and overcoming nervousness

Jade: health, healing, and perfection

Malachite: sleep and the heart's desire

Onyx: meditation, protection, and dispelling nightmares

Red jasper: grounding, inspiring friendship, and defending the home

Rose quartz: love, appreciation, peace of mind

Snowflake obsidian: protection, ending difficult times, and overcoming obstacles

Tiger's eye: looking beneath the surface and protection

Turquoise: health, friendship, and happiness

Spells box

As you become a more experienced sorceress, you will collect a variety of tools and objects that you'll use in your spellcasting. You should keep these objects in a special box, wrapped in silk or a material that's special to you.

Some of the items you may need are:

★ Candles ★ Compass ★ Crystals ★ Oil burner
★ Oils ★ Incense holder ★ Herbs ★ Paper
★ Fabrics in different colors, textures, and patterns
★ Scissors ★ Threads in various colors
★ Small containers for water, herbs, oils, salt
★ Special pen ★ Wand

The dedication

Give special power to the objects in your spells box with the following words:

Oh unseen powers of the universe,
I am taking my first step along the
path of knowledge.
Bless and charge these objects
with your strength.
Help me to use them
wisely and well.

Wand

You can cast successful spells without a wand, but using one will add power to your spells and energy when charging candles. Your wand should be no longer than your forearm. You could buy one from a wand specialist or even make one yourself using a special piece of wood that you feel a strong connection with. Invent your own wand incantations to supercharge your spellcasting.

The Sorcery Scene

Before spellcasting, turn off your cell phone, tidy up any clutter, and clear your mind of worries about homework or chores. Avoid objects that contain LED displays, such as digital radio alarm clocks. Remember, you are stepping aside from the ordinary world.

You will need a special space in which to perform your spellcasting. Choose a quiet, safe place where you will not be disturbed, one where you are allowed to burn candles. Your bedroom is probably the best spot to choose.

Special space

Prepare your special space before you begin each spell by following the steps below:

1. Brush or vacuum the area, focusing on cleansing and purity.
2. Once it is clean and tidy, sprinkle a few drops of water over the space.
3. Cover the area with a beautiful cloth, and meditate on the spells you will do in the future.

Dedicate special objects

Make sure that you have dedicated all your tools to the purpose of spellcasting, allowing your own energy to flow into them through meditation.

Purifying bath

Apart from being relaxing, a purifying bath cleanses your energy, so that you are able to achieve the best results from your spell.

Clothes

Set aside a special outfit that you will only wear during spellcasting. Many sorceresses choose to wear white, but you should wear a color and fabric that works with your energy. Above all, you should feel comfortable in it. If you wish, you can decorate your clothing with symbols that are meaningful to you.

Jewelry

If you want to wear jewelry, again, it should be meaningful to you. You give these items their energy, so the more important an item is, the more powerful it will be. Many sorceresses choose not to wear watches, because time is not important.

Ending your spellcasting

It is just as important to end your spells correctly as it is to begin them correctly. You have been acting as a channel for unseen energies. Those energies have to return to their natural home. Visualize them passing through you and returning to where they belong.

Preparing yourself

When you cast a spell, you should be in as pure a state as possible. This means cleansing your energy (your spiritual self) as well as your body (your physical self).

A purifying bath will clean both parts of you. Follow the steps below to perform a purifying bath. Ask an adult to help you with the candles and the oil burner.

You will need:

★ Large white candle
★ Second candle in a color of your choice
★ 2 drops rosemary oil, 3 drops lavender oil, 1 drop lemon oil (blended together well)
★ Glass of mineral water

Purifying bath

1 Burn the oil blend in an oil burner.
2 Run your bath, focusing on the water and thinking about the intention of the spell you are going to cast.
3 Light the white candle and then the colored one, and place them in safe places around the bathtub.
4 Get into your bath and relax. Halfway through your bath, drink the glass of water. Imagine it cleansing your body as you drink it.
5 Keeping your mind focused on your intention, safely snuff out the candles, and then get out of the bathtub.
6 Dry yourself with a white towel, then prepare to do some spellcasting.

Another way of cleansing is to shower, since it keeps the water flowing. As you shower, make a picture in your mind's eye of all impurities being washed away.

Creating the right atmosphere

When you are casting your spells, your surroundings can have a powerful effect on your success. Therefore, you must make sure that everything around you is working in harmony with your intention.

Space for your senses

Your special space should already be as you want it. But what about the area around your special space? If it is your bedroom, what does it look like? Is it messy, with clothes and books lying around everywhere? This could result in messy energies affecting your spell. Think about your five senses, and then look at your surroundings.

Sight

The colors and shapes around your special space should be harmonious and peaceful. Nothing should look uncared for, unclean, or messy. The energies of your surroundings affect your mood and therefore your spell. Make sure that all the things you can see make you feel content and happy.

Smell

The sense of smell is extremely powerful, and it is strongly connected with memory. If there are any negative aromas in your room, cleanse the area by burning incense or essential oils.

Taste

There should be no half-eaten foods around your special space, and you should avoid eating anything strong-tasting before performing your spell. The taste in your mouth should be pleasant, and you should not feel hungry or thirsty.

Touch

Just as the colors and shapes around your special space should give you a sense of peace, so should the feel of them. Harsh fabrics, unpleasant textures, and dusty or sticky surfaces will clog your energies and make it more difficult for your spells to work.

Hearing

If you live with other people or near a busy street, there will always be noises that could disturb you. This is why meditation is so important. If you can focus on the present and on your own actions, other sounds will fade into the background.

Time

The time of your spell can sometimes affect its success. Each day of the week has a unique energy and power. For each spell, decide which energy would suit you best, and cast the spell on that day.

* **Sunday:** ambition, fun, truth, and success
* **Monday:** emotions, dreams, and imagination
* **Tuesday:** courage, energy, protection, and confidence
* **Wednesday:** communication (including phone calls, emails, letters) and information
* **Thursday:** luck, wealth, and success
* **Friday:** dating, friendship, and love
* **Saturday:** tests, patience, and protection

The moon

The moon is a vital element of many spells. Look at
your diary; it may tell you which days of each month
will have a full moon. Otherwise, check online—there
are several moon phase calculators on the Internet.
Alternatively, keep looking up in the sky!

New moon

The new moon governs new wishes, love, and projects.
It is the best time to cast spells for new beginnings.

Waxing moon

This is when the moon seems to be growing. It is the
best time to give extra strength to spells that you have
already begun or to strengthen something that already
exists. It is a good time for luck spells.

Full moon

The full moon gives great magical power and is perfect
for healing spells. It is also a good time to charge
magical objects with extra energy.

Waning moon

This is the period when the moon seems to be
becoming smaller. It is the best time to cast spells that
want to lessen or remove something negative.

Spells for You

Your health, well-being, and happiness are more important than anything. You cannot be a successful sorceress if you don't take care of your own needs! One way in which you can do this is by casting spells for yourself.

Remember that you need to take good care of both your physical and spiritual selves. As you cast these spells, keep thinking about everything that makes you you—and what you like about yourself.

A good meditation to perform each morning is to stand in front of a mirror and breathe slowly in and out 10 times. Then look into your eyes and say aloud, "I like myself because . . ." Think of a new reason each day!

The spells in this section should be performed by you, for you. They are intended to encourage a peaceful mind, a healthy body, and a happy heart. Their success depends upon your state of mind and how strongly you wish the spell to succeed. Use them wisely and well.

A spell to give you a good night's sleep

Sometimes counting sheep just isn't enough! To achieve a good night's sleep, you need to be mentally relaxed. If your thoughts are whirling when you close your eyes, you will have a restless night full of disturbing dreams. In this spell, the state of mind of the spellcaster is extremely important.

Before performing this spell, do a meditation in your room. With your door closed, visualize a mirror on the outside of it. Now picture the mirror reflecting all negative energy away from you as you sleep. Focus on the image of your room as a safe, protected space.

Elements

★ Sprig of holly
★ Piece of malachite
★ Paper
★ Special pen

Time and Place

Perform this spell when you are ready for bed, after you have meditated.

✷Actions

1 Place the holly on your windowsill, and then sit on your bed, holding the piece of malachite. Think about all the things that are upsetting or worrying you. Don't get bogged down in the details; just identify what they are, making a mental list.

2 Now write down all the things you have thought of on the piece of paper.

3 Pass the malachite over the bed three times in a figure-eight pattern. This is the sign of eternity.

4 Wrap the paper around the malachite, and place it under your pillow, saying the incantation (below).

5 Go to sleep, and in the morning, hold the paper under running water, tear it up into small pieces, and then recycle it. Place the piece of malachite on your windowsill next to the holly.

👄 Incantation

Take away all cares and tears,
Slumber should be free from fears.
Holly and crystal grant good sleep,
With no more need for counting sheep.

43

A spell to encourage good health

1 First, think about water. Visualize clear, flowing water. Think about how it gives life to everything in the world. We are about 65 percent water, and we need it for our bodies to survive.

2 Next, think about food. Picture the vegetables that grow in the ground and the fruits that grow on trees. These are natural foods that give our bodies the vitamins they need.

3 Now think about your body. Visualize it running, jumping, cartwheeling, and stretching. Remember that it is the only body you have and that you must treat it with respect.

4 Finally, try to think about all three things at once, holding them together in your mind's eye. Now you are ready to perform the spell for good health.

Elements

★ 3 dried bay leaves
★ Paper
★ Special pen

⏲ Time and place

You should perform
this spell in your
special space at the
time of a new moon.

★ Actions

1 Write your precise wish for good health on the paper,
holding the above meditation in your mind.

2 Fold the paper into thirds, and put the bay leaves
inside it.

3 Visualize the things that you will need to do to
make the wish come true.

4 Fold the paper into thirds again, the other way,
then speak the words of
the incantation.

5 Hide the folded
paper in a safe,
dark place.

👄 Incantation

My body is the house of my spirit.
Just as I care for my special space,
So I will care for my body.
★
Grant me water, clear and sweet.
Grant me wholesome food to eat.
Grant me wisdom from above.
My body needs respect and love.

A spell to give you confidence

This is a spell that can only be performed by the spellcaster, on the spellcaster! It is a fun and energetic spell, full of noise and self-encouragement.

Having confidence is all about not worrying what others think of you. Before you start the spell, think about your friends and family. They are the people who matter, and they already like, love, and care about you very much. That thought should always boost your confidence!

Before you begin, decide on a one-line affirmation for yourself, or choose one of the affirmations below.

* I have the confidence to do anything.
* I am sure of myself.
* I can solve any problem.
* I have faith in myself.

Elements

★ Bell, rattle, or tambourine
★ Your favorite upbeat music

Time and Place

Perform this spell in the daylight, but choose a time and place where you will not disturb anyone else and where no one will interrupt you.

✷Actions

1 Play your music until you can feel the beat in your body like a heartbeat.

2 Dance around the room with your instrument, making as much noise as you can with it.

3 As you dance, call out your affirmation in a loud and positive voice.

4 Repeat the affirmation nine times as you continue to dance.

5 Repeat the spell once a week, and watch your confidence soar!

Feeling silly?

You may feel a bit embarrassed at first, but why worry? No one is watching! Let your fears go, and imagine the music carrying them away with its rhythm. Visualize the beat of the music drumming new confidence into you.

*A spell to control your temper

This spell will help you feel cool, calm and collected.

Concentrate on a time when you lost your temper. What triggered it? Are there certain words or actions that made you angry? Identify as many as you can.

⏰ Time and place

This spell should be performed in bright daylight when an adult is there to help you with the actions.

Next, think of a time when you felt peaceful and calm. Try to channel those feelings again. Close your eyes and visualize the time, place, and how good you felt. This state of mind is your goal.

Elements

★ Cup
★ Mint tea
★ Honey
★ Ordinary dark stone

★Actions

1 Ask an adult to prepare you a cup of mint tea, and start to breathe in the sweet aroma.

2 Visualize a circle of light around yourself. Hold the dark stone over the pit of your stomach. Think of all your anger flowing into the stone. Keep taking deep breaths.

3 Speak the first part of the incantation, concentrating on sending all your anger and negative energy into the stone.

4 Still holding the stone, carefully stir two spoonfuls of honey into the cooled mint tea, and say the second part of the incantation. Next, drink the tea, and visualize it flushing your last anger out into the stone.

5 Ask an adult to take you to a river, stream, or pond. Gently throw the stone into the water, saying the third part of the incantation.

Incantation

Part One
Take the furrows from my brow.
Ugly feelings leave me now.
Anger, temper, pass on through.
I have power over you.

Part Two
Mint to cool and clear my mind.
Honey sweet to cheer and bind.

Part Three
With this stone,
My anger's gone.
Waters flow,
And let it go.

A spell to be more assertive

Charm bags are a way of carrying a spell with you as a talisman. Whether you wish to be more assertive with friends or family, carrying a charm bag in your pocket as something you can touch will lend you great power.

Most people have felt shy at some point. Some people are so shy that it keeps them from saying what they think or feel. As you perform this spell, hold in your mind a time or place where you felt the most confident and sure of yourself.

To be a good sorceress, it is vital to truly know yourself. The more you know your own mind, the easier it will become to say what you think to others. Learning to be a sorceress will help you feel more confident and assertive.

Elements

★ Square of yellow fabric
★ Yellow ribbon
★ Ground nutmeg
★ Pine needles
★ Dried lavender

⏰ Time and place

You should perform this spell during the waxing moon, on your best day of power. Make sure that you are alone in your special space, but that an adult is nearby.

★ Actions

1 Put two pinches of nutmeg, one pinch of lavender, and three pinches of pine needles into the middle of the fabric square.

2 Next, use the ribbon to tie the edges of the square together and make a little bag. Tie a double knot and then a double bow. As you tie the ribbon, recite the incantation.

3 Wear the bag around your neck, or keep it in your pocket. Whenever you need to be more assertive, focus your mind on the charm bag. You should feel a surge of power and energy.

4 Every day for seven days, approach one new situation where you need to be assertive, drawing strength from the charm bag.

5 At the end of seven days, assess whether you still need the bag. If not, scatter the contents to all four compass points.

👄 Incantation

Double knots, be strong and hold.
Double bows, be brave and bold.
Charge this charm with
strength and fire,
For just as long as I require.

Spells
for
Home

A true home is a very magical place. It is a place where you feel safe and protected; it is a place that is filled with love. These qualities are exactly what a good sorceress needs for her base and refuge. However, every home sometimes goes through difficult times. There are many ways in which you can use your powers to improve the atmosphere and happiness of your home.

To maintain a truly happy home, you will need a great deal of respect and understanding for others and for yourself. It can sometimes be hard work, but until you hold these qualities in your heart, no spell you cast will work.

The spells in this section will teach you how to channel the energies of your home in a positive way. Your home is where most of your spellcasting will take place, so use these spells to fill it with love, peace, and power.

A spell to protect your home

Use this spell to give extra protection to your house, or use it to increase your own sense of safety when you are at home. Before you start, ground yourself and use a meditation to achieve a peaceful state of mind.

This is an enchantment to keep your home safe and deter those who mean harm. You and your family must also work together to maintain safety and peace.

Elements

★ Old key (look in old drawers, thrift stores, or antique markets)

★ Red ribbon

⏰ Time and place

You should perform this
spell in your house,
preferably before noon.

✱ Actions

1 Pick up the key in
your right hand, and hold
the red ribbon in your left hand.
Spend 60 seconds meditating on the things that make
your home happy.

2 Tap the door of the room you are in three times,
saying the incantation aloud.

3 Move on to the next door. Repeat this until you
have visited every door in your house.

4 String the key onto the ribbon, and tie up the
ribbon with a double bow.

5 Place the key in a
drawer in your kitchen
(the heart of the
house).

👄 Incantation

Lock in love and happy life.
Lock out danger, hate, and strife.
Lock in safety, lock in trust.
Turn all evil thoughts to dust.

A spell to restore peace in your house

There are many things that can cause a bad atmosphere in your house. Before you can restore a sense of peace, you must first understand what has caused the problem. While you are doing your spell, consider the solutions in your mind.

If there has been an argument, talk to the people involved. Ask what would need to happen for them to forgive the other person. If a visitor to the house is causing problems, focus on the reasons why that might be. Talk to them and find out if they're unhappy about something. In the case of accidents or breakages, think about how serious the damage is, how it will be fixed, and how long that will take—but remain positive.

Elements

★ Enough salt to fit into the cupped palm of your hand

★ Fireplace (or a white candle if you have no fireplace)

Time and place

Use the fireplace—or the warmest place in your house—when everyone is at home.

✦ Actions

1 Gaze into the flames of the fire (or candle flame). Think about the problem for 60 seconds. Focus on the events. What led to this situation?

2 For a further 60 seconds, think about the emotions that are bringing a bad atmosphere to the house. Are they anger, fear, hurt?

3 Speak the first part of the incantation.

4 Spend 60 seconds thinking about the solution to the problem. What is needed to restore peace?

5 Throw the salt onto the fire, speaking the second part of the incantation. If you have no fire, carefully sprinkle the salt around the candle, then snuff it out.

Incantation

Part One

Troubled times within these walls.
Peace and kindness breaks and falls.
Unseen powers, wisdom lend.
The time has come to
build and mend.

Part Two

Focus every thought and power,
To heal and soothe this very hour
Each troubled heart and
frowning face.
Set love and peace
within this place.

A spell to bless a new home

Almost everyone has experienced walking into someone's house for the first time and feeling either very uncomfortable or very at ease. This is because of the energies created by the people who live in the house. The more sensitive you are, the more you will be affected by the energies in a house.

For this reason, it is important to wash a new home clean of any old energies or events that could leave a bad impression. Your new home will then be cleansed and ready for a fresh start.

Ancient magic

A very old tradition states that the first things to be taken into a new home should be salt for wealth and bread for food. This will ensure that the people who live there will always prosper and have enough to eat.

Elements

★ Clean jar with a lid
★ White sage incense stick
★ Salt

⏰ Time and place

You should perform this spell
on the first night you spend
in the new house.

★Actions

1 Put a few pinches of salt into the jar, and light the incense stick.
2 Carrying the jar in one hand and the incense in the other; visit each room in the house.
3 Make a picture in your mind of the salt soaking up all negative energies.
4 Waft the incense smoke around the room, particularly the doors and windows.
5 Speak the incantation aloud.

👄Incantation

Unseen powers, cleanse and clear
Any pain that once was here.
Make this home feel fresh and new,
Inside out and through and through.
Protect this house and more beside;
Bless every living thing inside.

Spells for School

Has anyone ever tried to tell you that your schooldays are the best days of your life? It seems as if grown-ups forget what school was really like! Okay, school can be fun and happy. But it can also be full of worries, confusions, rivalries, jealousies, and challenges. The spells in this section will help you navigate through the times that aren't so great.

These spells are about improving your own ability to deal with situations at school. Sometimes you may wish to control the actions of someone who is upsetting you or a friend, but you must not give in to this temptation. A true sorceress knows that lasting change can only come from herself.

Charge your inner strength, and no one will be able to stand in your way!

Morning meditation

✳ Today will be better and brighter than any day before.
✳ I will move through the hours in love and forgiveness, relying on the vast strength I have within, as powerful and everlasting as flowing water.

61

✷A spell to bring success

This is a useful spell if you have to take any kind of test or face a difficult challenge. You'll probably find that you need it most often at school, but you can apply it to any situation.

Most spells require a certain amount of visualization, but it's especially important in this spell. Your visualization of success is the channel through which the unseen forces of the universe will pass to help you. Spend as much time as you can making the visualization clear and strong.

☕ Elements

★ Gold pouch (sew together two squares of gold fabric) ★ Green thread
★ Marigold petals ★ 1 tsp ground cinnamon
★ 1 tsp ground ginger
★ 1 tsp lemon peel
★ 3 drops bergamot oil
★ 1 small silver coin

⏰ Time and place

Cast this spell during the time of a waxing moon, outdoors on a sunny day. You should feel confident and safe in the place where you cast the spell.

✷ Actions

1 Visualize the exact type of success you require. If you want to win a sporting event, visualize yourself holding up the trophy. If you want to pass a test, visualize the marks you need written on a piece of paper. Spend as long as you can making a mental image of your success.

2 Mix all the ingredients together in a bowl. Then fill the pouch and tie the top with the green thread.

3 Hold the pouch up to the sun, as high as you can lift it, and speak the incantation.

4 Lay your pouch in the sun for an hour, so it can absorb the sun's rays. This should dry out the oil.

5 The pouch is now charged, and you should keep it with you at all times. Whenever you can, hold it up to the sun and visualize your moment of success.

👄 Incantation

Great sun, the source of strength and power,
Infuse this charm within an hour.
Success as bright as sunny rays,
Triumph crown my nights and days!

A spell to improve your brain power

Everyone goes through times when a subject or a project just seems too difficult, and you don't know where to start.

You might feel like giving up, but don't! You might not be having fun, but your brain likes to be tested!

This spell will not turn you into a genius overnight. However, it will make it easier for you to learn, and you will find that you understand things more quickly.

Elements

★ Gold tea light candle ★ Orange tea light candle ★ Yellow tea light candle ★ Cinnamon incense ★ Mint ★ Rosemary ★ Small bowl ★ 3 drops vanilla extract ★ Oil of your own choosing

Time and place

You should perform this spell at night, during a waxing moon. Make sure an adult helps you to use the candles safely.

★Actions

1 Put the candles in a line, with the gold candle in the middle, and light the incense.

2 Mix the mint, rosemary, oil, and vanilla extract together in a small bowl. Use your finger to rub a little of the mixture around the center of the candle.

3 Strike a match above the yellow candle, focusing on the unseen powers you are calling upon. Speak the first line of the incantation, and light the yellow candle.

4 Strike a second match above the orange candle, focusing on your ability to channel and absorb. Speak the second line of the incantation, and light the orange candle.

5 Strike a third match above the gold candle, focusing on your goal of brain power and intelligence. Speak the last line of the incantation, and light the gold candle.

6 Allow the candles to burn out. While they do, focus on improving your ability to learn.

👄 Incantation

I ask the unseen powers and forces of the universe to channel power into me.
Lend strength and clarity to my brain, help me to learn and absorb information as I absorb the unseen power.
May I reach my full potential in everything I do.

A spell to improve your memory and powers of concentration

Do you ever find your mind wandering in class? Is it sometimes difficult to remember everything you were taught? This spell will help you free your mind from distractions and focus on your schoolwork. It's especially helpful before tests and exams.

★ Elements

★ 2 pinches rosemary ★ 2 pinches basil ★ 1 pinch caraway seeds ★ 1 tsp lemon peel ★ Small purple fabric bag ★ Silver thread

Time and Place

You should perform this spell at a time of your own choosing.

✱Actions

1 Mix the herbs and the lemon peel together in a bowl while chanting the incantation.

2 Place the mixture into the bag.

3 Tie the bag with the silver thread.

4 Carry the bag with you at all times, and keep it in sight whenever you are working.

5 Whenever you need to concentrate, focus on the sachet, and you will be able to concentrate on your work.

6 Refresh your lucky bag every two weeks.

👄 Incantation

I call on the energies and power of words
To help me focus on the
wisdom they hold.
Let me use language with
thought and skill.
Remove confusion and
make me bold.

A spell to improve your attitude

It's hard to keep a positive mental attitude, especially if you're finding school a drag or having problems with friends or family. However, these are the times when a positive mental attitude is most important! It can help you get through the bad times and enjoy the good times even more.

This spell can only work if you are open to the positive possibilities. That means expecting the best, planning for success, and believing in yourself.

Elements
★ Paper
★ Special pen
★ Yellow tea light candle
★ Agate

Time and place
You should cast this spell during a waxing moon, when you are feeling at your strongest. Make sure an adult helps you use the candles safely.

✴Actions

1 Draw a horizontal line halfway down the piece of paper. Above the line write: Seize ✳ Truth ✳ Accept ✳ Respond
Below the line write: Defense ✳ Refusal ✳ Anger ✳ Guilt

2 Place the agate beside the candle, then light the candle. Speak the incantation, then pick up the agate and trace a figure eight over the paper with it, repeating the incantation a second time.

3 Hold the agate to your forehead and visualize all your negative, worried thoughts flowing out through the crystal and disappearing.

4 Allow the candle to burn out safely, and then stick the piece of paper to a mirror in your bedroom, where you will see it every day.

⬤Incantation

I will stay above the line.
Mistakes I make, I claim as mine.
I take control of my own life,
And fearless, face both
joy and strife.

Above the line

Remember, as long as you stay with the "S-T-A-R" qualities above the line, the unseen forces of the universe will help you stay positive. If you refuse to accept responsibility, you'll be filled with negative emotions. In fact, you'll be a total "D-R-A-G." So stay above the line, sorceress!

A spell to keep you calm for a long time

It is normal for your mood to change slightly from day to day. It can be affected by all kinds of things, including the weather, the moods of others, and your health. You cannot predict any of these things.

However, there are times when you know that you need to be calm and focused, for example, during exam week. This spell will help you to keep your energies in balance, and if your energies are balanced, you will feel better.

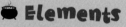

Elements

★ Bowl of water

★ Single white flower without a stalk

★ Green tea light candle

★ Yellow tea light candle

★ Jasmine incense

⏰ Time and place

It is good to cast this spell outside, as it links you with the earth. It should be performed in the light of day. Make sure an adult helps you use the candles safely.

⭐ Actions

1 Float the white flower in a bowl of water, meditating on its beauty.

2 Light the candles and incense, and think about the freshness and strength of nature.

3 Stand with your feet about 20 centimeters/8 inches apart, and think about your connection with the earth on which you are standing. Imagine energy rising up from the earth into you, through your feet.

4 Reach your arms up, and imagine energy moving down through your fingertips from the light.

5 Visualize the energies mingling inside of you, healing and balancing.

6 Say the incantation, and let the candles burn out.

7 Finish the spell by sitting quietly and imagining the calming energy at the center of your body.

💋 Incantation

Earth and light be mixed in me,
Fresh and calm as summer sea.
Keep me centered deep within,
Let a brand new day begin.

A spell to disperse gossip

When someone is gossiping about you, it can be very upsetting. First you must find out where the gossip is coming from. Who is spreading it? When you know this, you are already halfway to stopping it.

The next step is to forgive that person. It's hard, especially if they have been nasty to you. But the code of sorcery does not allow you to cast a spell in anger. Think about why they are spreading gossip.

Are they unhappy about something and trying to distract themselves? Have you upset them by accident, so they want revenge? When you understand the reason for their actions, it will become easier to forgive them. When you are calm and have truly forgiven the person, you may cast the spell.

Elements

★ Piece of paper that the gossip has touched

★ Box with a lid

⏰ Time and place

Perform this spell in your special space. Choose a day of the week when you are at your strongest.

✷Actions

1 Put the paper into the box. Close it tightly.

2 Hold the box with both hands, and speak the incantation.

3 Place the box in your special space, and surround it with white tea lights. Light them and meditate as they burn out. Think about the person and why they have been gossiping. Think about anything you have done to upset them by accident. Be honest with yourself!

4 When the gossiping has stopped, remove the paper from the box, and hold it under flowing water. Finally, tear it into tiny pieces. Now recycle them.

Incantation

Unseen powers, hear me say,
Gossip and anger take away.
Open up a path of peace
That love may win and
malice cease.

Spells for Friends

The friends that you make in life are like a family you choose for yourself. True friendship is a natural form of magic that needs no spellcasting. A genuine friend is always kind, always forgiving, always loving.

A friend may sometimes be angry with you, but they will be able to talk it through to forgiveness, and your friendship will grow stronger as a result.

You can use your magical energies to help your friends in ways they could not imagine, but remember, the spells in this section should be used with the full knowledge and permission of your friends. Being honest will bring you closer and you'll create a group of friends that will last a lifetime.

Friendship Meditation

* True friends are a gift from the world to me.
* I will spend time and energy on them.
* I will work hard to deepen and bind our friendship.
* Honesty, kindness, forgiveness and understanding, link us forever with the natural magic of love.

A spell to meet new friends

Imagine that you are in a house with all the lights turned off. People walk past, but they don't come to the door because they think no one is home. Attracting friends is like turning on a light inside the house and letting them know that you would like a visitor.

To attract new friends, your attitude is as important as the spell you cast. After you have performed this spell, you will meet people who are potential friends. However, you need to be able to recognize them, and that means looking outward and paying attention to those around you. Switch on your light!

Elements

★ 3 brown candles
★ Paper
★ Special pen
★ Gold thread

⏰ Time and Place

Perform this spell in your
special space. It will be
most powerful if you cast
it during a waxing moon.

✴ Actions

1 Light the candles carefully or ask an adult to help.
2 Write on the paper three qualities that you would
like a friend to have, and say each one aloud.
3 Fold the paper in half and hold it high above the
candles. Repeat the three words, speaking them at
the candle flames. The flame should flicker but
not go out.
4 Speak the incantation.
5 Snuff out the candles and wrap the paper around
them, tying it with the gold thread.
6 Keep the candles in a safe, dark place.

👄 Incantation

In my heart an empty space.
Bring a friend to fill that place.
Shine on me like glittering sun.
Double joy and double fun.

A spell to send positive energy

When your friend is going through a difficult time, you help and support them. You are there to listen to their worries and fears, to hold their hand when they need strength, and to defend them when they are weak. These are the foundations of your friendship, and they should be in place long before you cast any spells.

On top of this foundation, you have the power to give your friend magical support as well. This spell sends positive energy and encouragement to another person. It is a gift that you give, and your reward will be to see your friend feeling better.

Elements

★ Jade crystal
★ Frankincense oil
★ Oil burner

⏰ Time and Place

Carry out this spell in your special space at sunset, during a waxing moon.

✦ Actions

❶ Pour out some oil and light the burner.

❷ Carefully pass the crystal through the fumes from the burner three times.

❸ Face the direction where your friend is and say the incantation.

❹ Visualize a shell of energy building up around the crystal. Then place it beside your bed and picture the energy being directed towards your friend.

❺ Imagine the energy reaching your friend and surrounding them with a light of confidence.

❻ Next morning, wash the crystal under running water and then give it to your friend.

👄 Incantation

Unseen forces, brave and bright,
Send [friend's name] help and
strength tonight.
Give [him/her] the self-belief of youth,
Crowned with success
and throned in truth.

A spell to give power to a friendship

All friendships face challenges and tests, and sometimes it can feel as if your links with your friends are weakening. Usually this is because you have not been communicating with them enough. After you have cast this spell, plan to spend some time alone with each of your friends, doing something that you both enjoy.

This spell is not directed at a particular person, so you do not need to worry about getting permission. It is a way of strengthening existing friendships and encouraging new ones.

Elements

★ 2 pieces of paper
★ Special pen
★ 2 tsp almond oil mixed with 1 drop patchouli essential oil
★ White tea light candle

⏰ Time and Place

The best time to cast this spell is at the new moon, either outside or with a window open through which you can see the moon.

✴Actions

1 Rub a few drops of oil on the surface of the candle.

2 Carefully light the candle and then rub a little oil in to the inside of your wrists.

3 On one piece of paper, draw a picture of yourself. Underneath the picture, write down all the qualities that make you a good friend.

4 On the other piece of paper, draw some people and write down the interests and qualities you like to have in your friends.

5 Hold the papers together with the drawings facing each other and say the incantation.

6 Put a drop of oil on one corner of each piece of paper and allow the candle to burn out.

👄 Incantation

Friends meet, friends greet,
Companions all, kind and sweet.
Strengthen ties and fill each heart,
True friends never will depart.

*A spell to make up with a friend

Arguing with a friend is a very painful experience. You are upset because of the cause of the row, and because there is bad feeling between you and your friend.

Magic should never be used to force another person to act against their will. Therefore you cannot cast a spell to make your friend apologize. However, you can cast a spell to smooth the way towards making up.

Imagine that you and your friend are at opposite ends of a long path called forgiveness. If the path is blocked with overgrown briars and brambles, it will be very difficult for you to reach each other. This spell will help to clear the brambles out of the way, so that you can walk towards each other and meet in the middle.

Elements

★ Apple, cut in two
★ Piece of white paper, no bigger than the apple
★ Special pen
★ 2 cocktail sticks

⏱ Time and Place

Cast this spell during a waxing moon. It is best performed in the daylight and outside.

✴ Actions

1 Write your full name and your friend's full name on the piece of paper.

2 Place the paper between the two halves of the apple.

3 Visualize your friendship being healed. Think about what went wrong, and how it can be mended. Accept that you are responsible for the argument as well as your friend.

4 Insert a cocktail stick from right to left to pin the apple halves together, picturing yourself walking towards your friend with your hands held out towards them.

5 Insert the second cocktail stick from left to right, picturing your friend walking towards you with their hands held out towards you.

6 Send your love to your friend and ask to receive their love in return. You can then take the apple apart and dispose of the materials.

A spell to give protection to a friend

An umbrella gives protection from the rain. You might still get splashed with a few raindrops, but you won't get completely soaked. This spell gives your friend a sort of magical umbrella in times when they are feeling vulnerable or sensitive.

You can't protect them completely from the world around them, but you can keep the damage to a minimum, just like an umbrella does.

Elements

★ Rose quartz pendant
★ Long gold chain

Time and Place

This spell works over the course of a day and a night. It is best performed at the time of a waxing moon in your special space.

✳ **Actions**

1 As soon as you wake up, thread the pendant on to the chain and put it around your neck, under your clothes.

2 Three times during the day, and three times after sunset, take out the pendant and hold it in both hands as you say the incantation. Then kiss the pendant and return it under your clothes.

3 Wear the pendant all night. In the morning, give the pendant to your friend and ask them to wear it under their clothes, close to their heart.

4 Explain it is for their protection, and to show that you are thinking of them and care about them.

👄 **Incantation**

Protection for you,
From my heart to yours.
Faithful and true,
On seas and on shores.
Wrap you in cotton,
Defend you from harm.
Never forgotten,
I fill up this charm.

A spell to cheer up a friend

This simple spell is intended to lighten the heart of your friend and give them some happiness in a time of pain, sorrow or worry.

Friendship magic

Make sure that your friend knows that you are there to help and support them. Tell them how much you like them and why. You have learnt that listening is an important part of sorcery. If you listen to your friend's needs, you will always be able to support them.

Elements

★ Piece of card in a colour of your choice ★ Pen in a colour of your choice ★ Brown candle ★ Ylang ylang incense ★ Turquoise crystal ★ Envelope

⏰ Time and Place

You should perform this spell in your special space before midday at the time of a new moon.

✦ Actions

1 Light the candle and the incense, and meditate for five minutes, thinking about your friend and their state of mind.

2 Fold the card in half and on the front, draw the figure 8. This represents endless friendship and support.

3 Pass the crystal through the incense smoke three times, saying the incantation. Then place the crystal at the centre of the figure 8.

4 Visualize the worry and sadness leaving your friend and entering the crystal. Snuff out the candle.

5 Remove the crystal from the figure 8 and wash it under running water.

6 Write these words inside the card: Forever
Radiant
Inseparable
Encouraging
Necessary
Defender
Supportive

👄 Incantation

Take away sadness, take away sorrow.
Bring my friend a new tomorrow.
Unseen powers, hear this plea;
Let [friend's name] happier be.

7 Sign the card with love, place it into the envelope and give it to your friend.

*A spell to heal a friend *

Healing spells are an important part of magic. But here, healing does not just mean treating the cuts and grazes of your physical self. Spells can heal the emotional injuries of your spiritual self – your feelings and ideas.

If you are performing this spell to heal someone else, remember to first ask their permission. You will be sending out powerful healing energy, and it is important to treat it with respect.

Elements

★ Blue candle for healing ★ White candle for power ★ Pink candle for love
★ Rosemary incense
★ Clear quartz crystal
★ The name of the person to be healed written on a piece of paper

⏰ Time and Place

Healing spells are very powerful and this one should be cast under a new moon, in your special space. Make sure an adult helps you to use the candles safely.

★ Actions

1 Place the candles in a row, with the white candle in the middle. Put the incense on the left if the spell is for a girl, or on the right if it is for a boy. Carefully light the incense and the candles.

2 Put the paper with the name on it by the white candle, and place the crystal on top of the paper.

3 Visualize your own energy combining with the unseen energies of the universe. Enjoy the aroma of the incense. Take a few deep breaths and imagine your energy increasing with each breath.

4 When you feel ready, release your healing energy. Direct it through the crystal to the person you wish to heal.

5 Speak the incantation and then snuff out the candles.

👄 Incantation

[Name] be healed by this gift of power,
Growing stronger hour by hour.
Energy flow through every part,
May health and happiness fill your heart.

Spells for Luck

Luck and magic have been connected since time began. There are hundreds of tales of fairies, leprechauns and genies granting wishes or bringing bad luck upon humans. So it may come as a bit of a shock to learn that magic can't make luck.

Are you shocked? Don't be. Luck comes from your state of mind. If your head and heart are open and outward looking, you will start to notice the opportunities that surround you every day. If you are closed off, paying no attention to people or events, those chances will pass you by.

Before you perform any spell for luck, ensure that your state of mind is positive and healthy. Without that, no spell will work for you.

Luck Meditation

✳ I understand that luck is all around me.
✳ I can choose to be lucky or unlucky.
✳ I will hold my head high and keep my vision clear.
✳ I will draw luck to me like a ribbon of light,
    ✳ Wrapped around my heart.

*A spell to protect an object *

There are all sorts of occasions when you might wish to protect an object. Perhaps you are going on holiday and you want to make sure that your suitcase doesn't get lost. Maybe you are lending one of your most precious possessions to someone. Whatever the reason, this spell will help to keep an object safe from harm or theft.

Protective spells

There are spells that give protection for everything from your family car to your pets. As you become a more experienced sorceress, you will discover these and even create some of your own. Here are some of the associations of protective spells:

✳ **Best time:** waxing or full moon ✳ **Best day:** Sunday or Monday ✳ **Colours:** silver, white ✳ **Metal:** silver ✳ **Herbs:** rosemary, basil, nettle, garlic, laurel

Elements

★ Basil leaf
★ Silver ribbon
★ The object you wish to protect

★Actions

1 Place the basil leaf inside the object. If you can't, then rub the leaf gently over the object.
2 Rest your first and middle fingers on the object. Visualize a bright purple light streaming from your fingers and circling the object three times.

⏰Time and Place

You should perform this spell in your special space on a Monday. It will work best during a waxing moon, close to a full moon.

3 Weave the ribbon around the object.
4 Say the incantation three times.
5 Remove the ribbon and keep it in a safe place.

Incantation

Protected is this [object name] of mine,
Safe from danger for all time.

A spell to protect yourself on a journey

As a sorceress, you should always take steps to protect yourself from negative energies. However, there are times when you may need a little extra protection. This spell will protect you and your friends and family on a journey, but remember that a journey can be long or short. It could just be the walk to school!

A good protective spell should help to guide you away from danger and avert harm. For the spell to work well, you must stay alert and focused during your journey. If you meet a situation that makes you nervous, be sensible, follow your instincts and, if necessary, change your journey plan.

☕ Elements

★ 4 white tea light candles
★ Sandalwood essential oil ★ Basil
★ Rosemary ★ Sea salt
★ Clear quartz crystal ★ Silver coin
★ Square of dark blue fabric
★ White cord

⏰ Time and Place

Cast this spell at home, as close to your journey time as possible. Make sure an adult helps you to use the candles safely.

★ Actions

1 Run a bath, position the tea lights at the four corners of the bath, add the essential oil to the water and get into the bath.

2 As you lie in the bath, visualize the journey to come. Focus on the way you will travel, and create a mental picture of yourself arriving safely at your destination.

3 When you feel rested and relaxed, finish your bath and blow out the tea lights. (Relight them when you get home as a thank you for the safe journey.)

4 Place all the other elements onto the square of fabric and say the incantation.

5 Using the white cord, tie the cloth into a bag, and keep it close to you throughout your journey.

👄 Incantation

Let our lives protected be
Over land or over sea.
May this charm our health maintain,
Till we come back home again.

A spell to make a lucky charm

Almost any object can be a lucky charm, but it should be something that means a lot to you. For example, it could be a present from a friend, a family heirloom, a pebble you found on a happy day at the beach or a feather from a beautiful bird.

The energy that you put into your lucky charm will triple, and keeping it close to you will remind you that luck is something you can choose to draw upon!

Elements

★ Blue tea light candle
★ Rose incense
★ Mint leaves
★ The object you wish to turn into a lucky charm

⏰ Time and Place

Perform this spell in your special space on any day between the new moon and the full moon. Make sure an adult helps you to use the candles safely.

★ Actions

1 Carefully light the candle and the incense.

2 Hold the object in your writing hand and visualize energy travelling into your body – up from the earth and down from the sky.

3 Imagine the energy travelling to the palm of your writing hand and passing into the object.

4 Recite the incantation.

5 Gently rub the object with the mint leaves, and allow the candle to burn out.

👄 Incantation

I open my eyes to the chances around me.
Health and happiness, wealth and safety.
Energies flow and mingle here.
Let this [object name] attract good cheer.

A spell to encourage good weather

You should avoid trying to influence the weather too often. Nature knows what it's doing, and as a sorceress you should show it respect. However, for special occasions there are some ways to ask for fine weather.

Weather spells are difficult and your request may not always be granted. But for an extra-special day, it's always worth a try!

Elements
★ Gold candle
★ Red jasper crystal
★ Paper
★ Special pen

Time and Place

Before you decide to do this spell, think carefully, is it really vital to have good weather? If it is, you should perform the spell in your special space, a week before the date.

★ Actions

1 Draw a small map of the area where you want the sun to shine.

2 Carefully light the candle and move the map clockwise around it, three times. Focus on the flame, imagining that it is the sun.

3 Say the incantation, folding the paper in half each time you speak a line.

4 Place the folded paper on your windowsill, underneath the crystal, and snuff out the candle.

👄 Incantation

Fair winds blow and bright sun shine,
On this special day of mine.
Remember me a week today,
And send the rain clouds far away.

A spell to create opportunities

Luck cannot be forced, but opportunities can be made. You are surrounded by chances and opportunities every day. The more attention you pay to them, the more they will appear.

For this spell to be most successful, you should hold in your mind the kind of opportunities you want. Meditate on your wishes for some time before you cast the spell. Think about the chances that you wish to open up. Use your imagination to think of the possible ways these chances might come to you. Set your imagination free and let it soar!

Elements

★ Bowl of earth ★ Green bag (you can make this from a small square of fabric) ★ Paper ★ Needle and thread ★ Special pen ★ Cedar incense ★ Dried camomile ★ Mint essential oil ★ Honeysuckle essential oil

⏱ Time and Place

You should perform this spell
in your special space and
renew it every new moon.

✳Actions

1. Draw a picture of yourself and write your name underneath it. Keep concentrating on the opportunities you wish to draw towards you.
2. Put the camomile into the bag and add a few drops of oil. Then sew the bag shut.
3. Carefully light the incense and hold the bag in the smoke, speaking the incantation. As you speak, run your fingers through the earth in the bowl.
4. Keep the bag safe among your possessions – perhaps on your dressing table or in your bag.

👄 Incantation

Force of chance please work for me,
Guide me to opportunity.
Part of the nature, part of earth,
Let me win what I am worth.

A spell to find a lost object

Everyone loses things sometimes – even the most experienced sorceresses! Objects roll under sofas or fall between cracks in the floorboards. Belongings are left at friends' houses or dropped in the street.

Whatever you have lost, this is a simple and fast-working spell to help you find it again. It is important to remember that this is a spell to locate lost objects. It should never be used on people or anything living.

Elements

★ 3 green tea light candles
★ 1 gold tea light candle
★ Picture of what is lost or something that symbolizes it.

⏰ Time and Place

This spell should be performed in your special space, and works best during a full moon. Make sure an adult helps you to use the candles safely.

✳ Actions

1. Carefully light the green candles, reciting part one of the incantation as you light them. In between lighting each candle, turn on the spot, clockwise.
2. Place the gold candle closest to you, near the picture of what is lost.
3. Concentrate on the item you have lost and recite the second part of the incantation as you light the gold candle.
4. Wait for the candles to burn out and then the spell will start to work.

Incantation

Part One
Turn this object's fate around.
What is lost shall now be found.

Part Two
To unseen powers I apply:
Give guidance to my inner eye.
Show me what I need to find,
Relieve the worry on my mind.

Spells for Love

Love and magic go together like the stars and the moon. For hundreds of years, people have searched for love potions to make a friend adore them, love spells to identify their soul mate, or love charms to make a lost sweetheart return to them.

Remember: A true sorceress would never force anyone to do something they don't want to do. That goes against the essence of the magical code. However, you can use your magical energies to help you find your way along the path of true love. The spells in this section will teach you to listen to your own heart—and to the hearts of others.

These spells are all about learning to see with the eyes of your mind and helping others to do the same. When you feel better about yourself, you will feel more confident around others. And happy, confident people are attractive!

Love meditation

✳ When I am in love, I open up my heart.
✳ I am sensitive and easily hurt.
✳ I will remember that others
feel the same.
✳ I will be careful of their feelings,
as if I were holding their
heart in my hands.

A spell to dream of your true love

This is a spell that allows the caster a brief peek into the future. Again, although it can be an interesting and sometimes illuminating spell, it should not be taken too much to heart. Unless you are an expert dream interpreter, understanding the symbols used in your sleep is very difficult.

Elements

★ 3 white sugar-covered almonds

⏰ Time and place

You can only perform this spell once a year, on the evening of February 13th, and you should perform it in your special space. This is the eve of Saint Valentine's Day, and it is a night that shimmers with powerful energies. Before casting the spell, make sure you are well grounded (see page 10).

✶Actions

1 Open your window, and breathe in the night air deeply. Imagine yourself breathing in energy and breathing out tiredness and sadness.

2 Hold the three almonds in your writing hand, and recite the incantation.

3 Place the almonds beneath your pillow, then change into something white.

4 Focus only on yourself as you drift off to sleep.

●Incantation

Almonds sweet and wholesome three,
Show me who my love will be.
Let me glimpse in all or part
Where the future guides my heart.

✶Alternative spell

This spell is not as powerful, but you can use it at any time of the year.

1 Looking into a small mirror, stare deeply into your eyes. Without blinking, recite the words:

Glass of wisdom, let me see
Who my heart's true love will be.

2 Put the mirror under your pillow. Do not blink until it is hidden.

3 Go to sleep and prepare to dream of love!

A spell to get noticed

This spell is simple and quick, but just like all spells, it is important to prepare carefully. Make sure that you are grounded and that your head and heart are both at peace before you attempt it.

This is an enchantment to draw others toward you in a positive way—it doesn't mean that you will always want to be noticed by the people you attract! It's important to remember the love meditation from the start of this chapter. You should always be kind to the people who pay attention to you.

Elements

★ Circle of rose-pink fabric
★ Yellow ribbon
★ Petals from your favorite flower
★ Small, red paper heart
★ Bright coin

⏰ Time and place

Perform this spell in your special space at night, during a full moon.

✳ Actions

1 Place the fabric circle in front of you on the ground or on an empty table.

2 Keeping your eyes on the circle, spend one minute in meditation, thinking about the type of person that you want to attract.

3 One by one, put the petals, heart, and coin on the fabric. As you place each item, think of one characteristic of the type of person that you want to attract.

4 Tie the fabric into a pouch with the yellow ribbon using seven knots. As you tie the knots, chant the incantation.

5 Hang the pouch beside your bed, so that it is close beside you when you dream.

👄 Incantation

Seven knots for open eyes.
Seven knots inducing smiles.
Seven knots to let them see.
Seven knots to noticed be.

A spell to meet a soul mate

This is a spell that will draw a soul mate toward you. It is not to be cast on or about a particular person. Done well, it will attract love to you. It should be performed with a free and happy heart. If you are discontented, upset, or angry, it simply won't work.

Remember that happiness attracts happiness. Love attracts love. The more loving you are toward your family, friends, and pets—even your plants!—the better this spell will work.

Before you begin, use your meditation time to think about what love means to you and what a soul mate might be like.

Elements

★ Small box ★ Red pen ★ Vanilla incense ★ Dried rosemary ★ Rose quartz crystal ★ Pink tea light candle

✴Actions

1 Write "Love is mine" in red on the box.

2 Light the incense, then put the crystal and the rosemary in the box.

3 Put anything else that reminds you of love into the box, such as poems or heart-shaped candies. Don't put anything into the box that makes you think of a particular person.

4 Imagine yourself being happier than you have ever been! Now light the candle and say the incantation.

5 Snuff out the candle, then add it to the box.

6 Allow the incense to burn out, then shut the box. You must not open it again until you have met your soul mate. At that time, take the crystal out of the box and keep it safe. Bury the box in some earth.

⏰Time and place

Sit in a your special space to perform this spell, at a time when you feel at your best—powerful and relaxed.

⬤Incantation

Love I give
And love I seek.
Bring to me
A love unique.

A spell for making up

When you have argued with a friend or loved one, the air between you is dark and heavy. This spell is intended to help clear the air, but you must be very careful. It will give you the chance to talk and heal your relationship. But it may be that your relationship cannot be mended. Either way, this spell will give you both the chance to understand how each other feels.

Before you cast the spell, ground yourself and think about what has gone wrong between you and the other person. Try to be honest with yourself. Are you responsible for any of the problems? Accept that there may be things you could have done better, and be willing to learn what they are.

Elements

★ Magnifying glass
★ Photo of the other person

⏰ Time and Place

Perform this spell in your special space. It should be cast at night—before midnight and under a new moon.

⭐ Actions

❶ Place the magnifying glass over the photo of the person's face.

❷ Speak to the magnified picture about your feelings and wishes. State what you think the other person can do to make you feel better. Do not cast blame or get angry. Simply say how you feel and what you think the solution might be.

❸ Step away from the magnifying glass, and speak the incantation.

❹ Remove the glass from the picture, and replace the photo where it came from.

❺ Visualize your message darting through the sky toward the other person, and imagine yourself soaring above it as you go to sleep.

👄 Incantation

Here I stand, this spell I do
To clear the air between us two.
In a mood that's kind and calm,
Teach me how to heal this harm.

A spell to ease a broken heart

If you have had your heart broken, you know that it is almost unbearably painful. Physical wounds heal quickly, but a broken heart can seem to last forever.

No spell can completely heal a broken heart. Only time and patience can do that. But this spell will help to make it easier to bear.

Above all, do not hold on to anger, jealousy, or bitterness. These emotions will cloud your magical abilities and make you weak. This spell works by making you feel better. The happier you feel, the easier it is to forgive and let go of the past.

Elements

★ 1 strawberry teabag ★ Sea salt ★ 2 pink candles ★ Mirror ★ Pink drawstring bag ★ Quartz crystal ★ Copper coin ★ China bowl ★ 1 tsp dried jasmine ★ 1 tsp strawberry leaves ★ 10 drops apple blossom oil ★ 10 drops strawberry oil

⏰ Time and place

You should perform
this spell at home on
a Friday morning
or evening.

✴ Actions

1 Ask an adult to make
you a mug of strawberry tea.
2 Run a bath and pour some
sea salt into it. Then light one pink candle, and take
your bath in its light.

3 When you have dried off and dressed, sip the tea.

4 Brush your hair, breathe deeply, and relax. Now
place all the other ingredients on a table, then light
the second pink candle.

5 In the bowl, mix together the oils and herbs. As you
stir, look at yourself in the mirror while speaking
the incantation.

6 Put half the potion in the bag with the coin and
crystal, and carry the bag with you.

7 Leave the other half of the
potion in your special
space.

8 Repeat this spell every
Friday for as long as
you need to.

👄 Incantation

Unseen powers, rise and flow,
Protect my heart, which sinks so low.
Help me through these heavy days,
Guide me to lighter, happier ways.

A spell to peek into the future

Crystal balls, tarot cards, palm reading … for as long as anyone can remember, people have been trying to catch a glimpse of the future. At the very best, you can only hope to see a tiny flash of the future. Even then, you may not interpret it correctly. So don't put all your trust in what you see; instead, cast the spell with a happy, light heart, and have a little fun!

First, you must decide what subject you wish to know more about. How far into the future do you wish to peer? Do you have a particular question to ask? Make sure you know what it is you want to discover. It is especially important to take a purifying bath before casting this spell.

Elements

★ Square of sky-blue fabric ★ Ash leaves
★ Bay leaves ★ Holly leaves
★ Jasmine petals ★ Rose petals
★ Marigold flowers ★ Gold cord
★ White paper
★ Special pen

⏰ Time and place

You should perform
this spell in your house,
preferably before noon.

✳ Actions

1 Lay out the fabric, then put the ash leaves, bay
   leaves, rose, holly, jasmine petals, and marigold
   flowers in the middle of the cloth.
2 Bring the corners toward the middle. Tie them
   together like a small bag with the gold cord.
3 On the paper, write as clearly as you can what you
   wish to find out about the future.
4 Place the herbal bag and the note beneath your
   pillow, speaking the incantation.
5 Go straight to bed. Your dreams will bring you the
   answer to your question. As soon as you wake up,
   write the dream in your dream journal.

Incantation

Sweetest sleep and inner sight,
Bless my magic dreams tonight.
Let me know what lies ahead,
While I slumber in my bed.

Spellwriting

Now that you have worked through the book and tried some of the spells, you are a few steps further along on your journey to become a sorceress. However, there is one vital skill you need to practice in creating your own spells.

Every good sorceress knows that the finest spells are tailored for you. You will get the best results from certain herbs, colors, crystals, and times. Get into the habit of writing down the spells you do and what the results are. When you look back through your notes, you will see which elements are most effective for you.

A spell is made up of many parts, and you will need to think about them all when you start writing your own spells.

Spell checklist:

✳ **Intention:** What are you aiming to achieve by casting your spell?
✳ **Elements:** What ingredients and tools will you need to make it work?
✳ **Time:** What day, time, and moon phase will you work the spell in?
✳ **Place:** Where will you work the spell?
✳ **Actions:** What steps are needed to cast the spell?
✳ **Incantation:** What words will you chant?

Intention

The intention behind your spell is vital to its success and to your safety. Remember the rule of three—a spell can rebound on you with three times the power. The first step in writing a spell is to clearly state what you want it to do. To help you, work through this list of questions (and be honest!). If you answer "no" to any of them, you should put this spell to one side and come back to it at a later date.

★ Do your physical self and your spiritual feel balanced?

★ Have you eaten and drunk enough to satisfy your body's needs?

★ Have you meditated on the need for this spell?

★ Does this spell leave others free from your control?

★ If you are casting this spell for or about someone else, do they know about it and agree to it?

★ Are you properly grounded and in a positive mood?

Elements

Look back at the Spell Supplies chapter (page 18). You will find information about all the elements you might need for basic spellcasting. However, those are not the only ingredients and tools you can use. The elements you choose to put into your spells are up to you.

Search inside ...

Look around your home and possessions. Are there any meaningful ornaments, fabrics, or objects that could be useful in a spell? Visit the kitchen—explore the aromas of the herbs and spices you will find there. Do you feel connected to any of them?

... and out!

Walk around your neighborhood. Keep looking for natural items that could be used in your spells. Leaves, shells, flowers, pebbles, twigs . . . the possibilities are out there, just waiting for you to discover them!

Time

The time at which you cast a spell should be chosen wisely and well. You have learned a little about days of power and about the phases of the moon. There is much more to know, but for now, this simple checklist will help you. It provides a summary of the things you have discovered.

1 Upon which day should your spell be cast for the most powerful effect?

2 Should the spell be cast at night, in the light of the moon? Or would daylight be better? Trust your instincts with this question—some spells will suit the daylight, and some will harmonize better with shadows.

3 Which phase should the moon be in during this spell? If you are uncertain, think about your spell's intention, and then read about the moon phases again (see page 39).

 Place

You have a special space in which most spells can be performed well. However, there are times when a spell might require the light of the sun, fresh air, or the flowing water of a stream. As you develop your magical skills, seek out places where you feel comfortable both inside and outside your home. Make sure that you are completely safe and that an adult is always nearby when spellcasting outdoors.

Many sorceresses choose to set up a permanent spellcasting area in their special space. To do this, you will need to dedicate special items and keep them there.

Special spell supplies

1 Two candles with candleholders.
2 An incense holder.
3 A small case for flowers or herbs.
4 A small bowl or cauldron.

✳ Actions

The actions or steps of a spell will seem quite natural after you have been spellcasting for a little while. You will find it easy to decide on the steps you wish to take. Here are a few tips to help you as you begin writing your own spells.

1 Keep your spells as simple as possible—the more complicated you make them, the more things can go wrong.

2 The most powerful spells are often the most quick and easy to cast.

3 If you have more than ten steps, you're making it too complicated!

Remember that the details of each spell are crucial. If a candle needs to be snuffed out or allowed to burn out, make sure you record it. When you come to the spell again, you may not remember everything unless you write it down.

Incantation

The incantation should humbly ask the unseen powers of the universe to assist your spell. You do not control them, and you must show them respect. All universal energies, living things, and creations of nature deserve your respect.

It often helps if your incantation rhymes. This is because a rhyme is musical and has rhythm. It sounds beautiful and polished. Like you, the energies you are calling upon respond best to beauty.

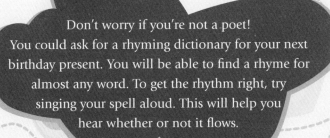

Don't worry if you're not a poet! You could ask for a rhyming dictionary for your next birthday present. You will be able to find a rhyme for almost any word. To get the rhythm right, try singing your spell aloud. This will help you hear whether or not it flows.

✳ Book of Spells ✳

No sorceress is complete without her book of spells. This is a volume in which she records all her most successful spells. Follow these steps to make your own unique spell book.

★ Choose a large, blank notebook with thick pages. Pick out a special pen and dedicate it to spellwriting. It is best if you use a fountain pen with ink cartridges.

★ Sit quietly in your special space with the notebook in your lap. Meditate on the future spells that will be written on its pages. Visualize yourself writing many positive, healing spells.

★ Imagine the notebook crammed with positive energy, which flows from your hands into its pages and back into your body again.

★ Say the words:

I dedicate this book to the unseen powers that guide me.
Flow through these pages and lend strength
and wisdom to my spells.
May I stay grounded and yet soar
among the stars.

★ When you begin writing, start each spell on a fresh page, and write down every tiny element of the spell.

★ Decorate the pages of the book in a way that is personal to you. If you are artistic, illustrate the pages with your own pictures and symbols. You could cut pictures out of magazines, stick feathers and fabrics on the pages, or even paint symbols on the pages in watercolor or oil paint.

★ Each time you close the book, say "I close these pages with peace and happiness."

★ Each time you open the book, say "I open these pages with love and good intentions."

★ Wrap the book in white fabric, then tie it in a single bow with a piece of silver cord.

Happy spellcasting!